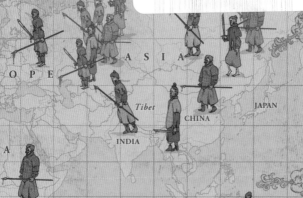

A S I A

O P E

Tibet

INDIA

CHINA

JAPAN

A

Indian Ocean

AUSTRALIA

ZOMBIES AT WAR

THE
ART OF WAR
for
ZOMBIES

Ancient Secrets of World Domination
~~APOCALYPSE~~ EDITION

Sun-Tzumbie
Translated and annotated by
Madame Cadavre Exquis

Interpreted by Rene J. Smith
and Virginia Reynolds
Illustrated by Bruce Waldman
Cartography by David Lindroth

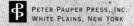
Peter Pauper Press, Inc.
White Plains, New York

DEADICATION

To our newest Undead recruits.
Good moaning! Today is the first day
of the rest of your afterlife.

Designed by Margaret Rubiano
Illustrations copyright © 2011 Bruce Waldman
Map copyright © 2011 David Lindroth, Inc.

THE
ART OF WAR
for
ZOMBIES

Ancient Secrets of World Domination

APOCALYPSE EDITION

CONTENTS

PUBLISHER'S NOTE

Written by Chinese philosopher general Sun Tzu in the 6th century BC, *The Art of War* is the definitive work on military strategies. Popular today also in the fields of business, sport, law, and education, which embrace the strategy of adapting to changing conditions, *The Art of War* has been published worldwide for centuries and has sold millions of copies.

Now, for the first time adapted by Sun-Tzumbie for use by the Zombie community, subsequently translated and annotated by Madame Cadavre Exquis, and modernized by Rene J. Smith and Virginia Reynolds, *The Art of War for Zombies* is unearthed and in print. This text is essential reading for the Undead in the coming Zombie apocalypse.

PREFACE

Sun-Tzumbie vanished in the year 918 BA (before apocalypse), soon after committing his famous text to paper. He is believed to be Undead and in seclusion in a remote area near the border of Tajikistan and China. Sightings have been reported in China, Uzbekistan, and as far south as Kashmir, but these cannot be corroborated. The text in this volume was recovered in the year 1871 during one of my many Asian expeditions. All porters were subsequently eaten. I translated and annotated Sun-Tzumbie's (incomplete) manuscript with the help of Undead scholars in St. Domingue, Transylvania, and New Orleans. Any errors or omissions are mine.

Madame Gadame Exquis

Cap-Haïtien, Haiti, 1958

INTRODUCTION

They walk among us: The Living. And they have for centuries. They are the Human Race—our nemesis. They seek to vanquish us. But we bite back. Still, every Zombie needs support. Hence this book.

The Art of War for Zombies will assist you, Undead Comrade, on your journey through the land of the Living. Based on the teachings of Sun-Tzumbie, with additional anecdotal material from Madame Cadavre Exquis, this book will help the Horde become organized as it reveals ancient Zombie secrets for overcoming our Living opponents.

Discover how to assess your Enemy, plan for sieges, and develop offensive strategy (an easy task for us of the decaying flesh). Understand that female Humans *will* wear high-heeled shoes during Zombie outbreaks, making them easy targets. (Why do Humans insist on thinking the Apocalypse is going to be sexy?) Laugh because a popular "Zombie survival manual" is dispensed *not* in bookstore "Self-Help" sections, but in "Humor." BWAHAHA! (Unfortunately, it remains a bestseller.) And remember: Those who do not learn from history are condemned to repeat it. Soon every day will be the Day of the Dead. If you can't join 'em, beat 'em—and eat 'em!

As Sun-Tzumbie says, "If you know the Enemy and know yourself (or what's left of you), you need not fear the result of a hundred battles."

It all starts by declaring one word:

WAR.

THE APOCALYPSE
WILL NOT BE
TELEVISED.

one

LAYING PLANS

DEAD RECKONING

Or, how zombies will win the day

Sun-Tzumbie said: The art of war is of vital importance to the Horde. War is a matter of life and death, or undeath, as we prefer. It is a road either to safety or to ruin. Hence it is a subject of inquiry which can on no account be neglected. If we are to take over the world, we must have a plan. Yes, we are Zombies. Planning is not our strong suit. However, with a little effort and a lot of BRRRAAAIIINNNS (*NOM NOM NOM*), we will prevail.

THE FACTORS OF WAR

While Humans will be hampered by their insistence on following their pesky laws and leaders, we are Zombies. The Horde is under no such constraint. Immoral law wins the day. We are only dismayed by danger inasmuch as we fear a crowbar to the eye socket. That is to be avoided.

Our goal is to create Hell on earth. Unlike our puny Mortal antagonists, we are unfazed by variations in seasons, temperature, wind, and precipitation. (Ever notice how much Humans whine about the weather? Pathetic!)

Yes, Earth will soon be ours. We have the ability to traverse great swaths of the planet (albeit slowly), while Humans are constantly stopping to check their messages or their makeup, to re-load, or to refuel their soon useless vehicles. Short of removing miscellaneous body parts, there is little they can do to stop us. Take heart! Take brain! Take kidney!

The Undead individual shows itself superior in every respect. While Humans look to their leaders, in the Horde it's every corpse for itself. We don't need no stinkin' commander. Except when we do. However, we can become a well-oiled, brain-eating machine by following a few simple rules. Within the Horde, there are ranks and classifications. The Zombie who knows its place in the Horde will be victorious. Feed off the instincts, and other bits, of your comrades. Control of the supply chain—BRRRAAAIIINNNS, BRRRAAAIIINNNS, and more BRRRAAAIIINNNS—is crucial, as is knowing our terrain, because we're not always too steady on our feet. We cannot allow the Humans to press their advantages.

DETERMINING THE ADVANTAGE

To assess the Zombie advantage by judging the military conditions, consider:

Which of the two beings—Zombie or Human—is less hampered by moral law? Um, is this question necessary? Completely devoid of higher brain functions, including that pesky conscience, the Zombie is clearly favored in this arena.

Which of the two has the most ability—a Human Mortal or the Undead? This depends on how you define the concept of "ability." We have the ability to terrorize every Living, breathing Human. How badass is that? Reasoning ability? Not so much, but who cares when you're badass? In the meantime, our foes are still struggling with the question, "How do you kill something that's already dead?" Human FAIL.

With whom lie the advantages derived from Hell on Earth? We created it. We control it. BWAHAHA!

On which side is discipline most rigorously enforced—Human side or Zombie side? We need to do a little work in this area, which is why we created this book on your behalf. Our Enemies tend to fall into phalanxes fairly easily; however, our superior numbers and endurance allow us to easily overcome them under most circumstances.

Which army is stronger—Human or The Horde? Humans have learned very little about Undead behavior from their movies and games. *Zombie Strippers? Plants Versus Zombies?* Please. They see us as "entertainment," even as "zomedy." A fatal flaw. They underestimate us at their own peril.

On which side are officers and soldiers more highly trained: the Human side or the Zombie side? Team Zombie is on autopilot, 24/7. We do one thing, and we do it well: *We hunt down and eat Humans. We are BRRRAAAIIIN-eating machines.* Humans may do impressive things with modern equipment, military Zombie kits, even toilet lids and crowbars, but they cannot withstand our unending onslaught and quest for Gray Matter.

In which army is there greater constancy both in punishment and in reward? In the Horde, punishment is simple. In fact, there is only one capital punishment—getting decapitated. The sentence is carried out swiftly, without your remorse, and probably without your conscious knowledge. You won't know what hit you.

Your reward is equally simple:
BRRRAAAIIINNNS,
glorious BRRRAAAIIINNNS.

By means of these seven considerations we may forecast victory or defeat. So, Zombie Nation, hearken to my counsel and conquer. The Undead who hearken not to my counsel will suffer defeat—let such a one be dismissed! Zombie FAIL.

ALL WARFARE IS BASED ON DECEPTION.

*Zombies, when able to attack,
should strive to appear unable, and shamble
about in seeming disarray.*

*When using our forces, we must
take care to seem slow-witted and incapable.
(Yes, we are naturally proficient
in this department.)*

*When we are near, we must make the Enemy
believe we are far away. When we are far away, we
must make him believe we are near.*

*Hold out baits to entice the Enemy.
Cupcakes work well, as does bacon.*

*Feign disorder, and crush him. Nobody takes
Zombies seriously, and for this they will pay.*

If he is secure at all points, be prepared for him. Dismembered body parts can be used as weapons. Chew on this: Even your severed head can deliver a coup de grace!

If he is in superior strength, evade him. Given our legendary endurance, this is a no brainer. Bodies of water are to be avoided, however (see page 96).

If your opponent is hot headed and high-strung, seek to irritate him further. Note: His digestive tract will likely be unappetizing.

Pretend to be weak, that he may grow arrogant. They never learn, do they? And they say we're the dumb ones.

If he is relaxing, give him no rest. If his forces are united, separate them. Divide and devour.

Attack the Human where he is unprepared, appear where you are not expected. Press this advantage at every turn. Nothing unhinges a Human more than a Zombie outside an open window.

All this strategizing aside, Horde tactics are driven by one directive and one directive only:

WORLD DOMINATION.

Brains

two

WAGING WAR

The race is not
to the swift,
nor the battle to
the ambulatory

B. Waldman

Sun-Tzumbie said: *In the operations of war, where there are in the field a thousand swift Rams, Raptors, and PT Cruisers, as many heavy Hummers, and a hundred thousand chainsaw-carrying Humans, the expenditures for essentials— including ammunition, armor, entertainment of guests, and small items such as Yodels and beer—will reach untold amounts each day.* Such is the Humans' cost of raising an army of willing soldiers.

Our cost: nada. The Zombie need not raise a levy, nor use sport utility vehicles. Or weapons, uniforms, or even clothing, for that matter. Clothes do not make the Zombie.

Zombies, you bring war material with you—your terrifying Virus, your vicious bite, your overpowering odor. You may forage—literally—on the Enemy. Thus the Horde should have BRRRAAAIIINNNS enough for its needs. Certainly enough to carry out the first principle of waging war: Bleed 'em dry!

Three noblemen encounter three cadavers. A popular theme of medieval art, "living meeting dead" was intended to warn the living of their coming mortality, and cause them to repent.

The Humans will become impoverished. The proximity of a Zombie army will cause scarcity of resources, high prices, and widespread panic. The Humans' substance will be drained away. The peasantry will be afflicted by heavy exactions. They will panic, squabble over tubular snack foods and can openers, and slow each other down. Yes, they will seem brain dead, but rest assured—there is juicy Gray Matter inside each and every one.

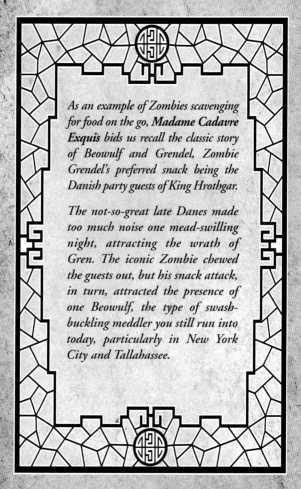

As an example of Zombies scavenging for food on the go, **Madame Cadavre Exquis** bids us recall the classic story of Beowulf and Grendel, Zombie Grendel's preferred snack being the Danish party guests of King Hrothgar.

The not-so-great late Danes made too much noise one mead-swilling night, attracting the wrath of Gren. The iconic Zombie chewed the guests out, but his snack attack, in turn, attracted the presence of one Beowulf, the type of swash-buckling meddler you still run into today, particularly in New York City and Tallahassee.

Beowulf tore off Grendel's arm, and though our Gren escaped, the wound weakened him sufficiently to cause his ultimate demise.

Note that later on, Beowulf (may he rot in Hell!) cut off Grendel's head and returned it to King Hrothgar. Ultimately, however, karma bit back: After Beowulf went on to destroy Grendel's avenging mother (yes, this truly is a heart-rending story!), the swordslinger himself was destroyed by a dragon. His final destination: the funeral pyre.

With war causing loss of substance and exhaustion of strength, the homes of Humans will be stripped bare. Their income will be dissipated; their gas-depleted Silverados and Siennas will rust. Nonfunctioning generators, chain saws, and leaf blowers will accumulate.

Hence a wise Zombie general makes a point of baiting the Enemy. One abandoned Costco, because of its power to tempt Humans with pallets of still-edible Dinty Moore and bins of Lance Honey Buns,* is equivalent to 20 Whole Foods Markets (with their way-beyond-the-sell-by-date moldy fuzz-plosions of Arugula That Time Forgot).

When Humans engage in actual fighting, if victory is long in coming, they will weary of wielding their fire extinguishers and toilet lids and their ardor will be dampened. If we lay siege to their malls, their radioactive landscapes, their Dixie swamplands, and their theme parks, they will exhaust their strength. If the campaign is protracted, the resources of the Humans will not be equal to the strain.

We must, however, strike a balance between wearing down the enemy, and wearing down ourselves. Though we have heard of stupid haste in war, cleverness has never been associated with long delays. We are, of course, shambling as hastily as we can, but let's face it—we are not that clever, delays or no delays.

And yet, despite the fact that there is no instance of a country having benefited from prolonged warfare, delays can serve our own Zombie Nation quite well. Thanks to our ingenious recruiting program, our victims become our soldiers! We may also dig up additional ready recruits at a convenient graveyard.

*Speaking of snack foods, let Zombies adopt the former slogan of a prominent American snack food company: "Don't go 'round hungry."

The nature of the Human is such that in order to kill their Enemy (namely us), they must be roused to anger. In addition to the obvious advantage (such as life) of defeating the Horde, they must also have "rewards," even if these consist of unlimited rides on the Tilt-A-Whirl and looting tourist souvenir shops.

Zombies must be roused, period. Generally by movement, noise, and proximity of meat (i.e., the reward).

Therefore in attacking HOV-lane cars and trucks, also known as Meals on Wheels, when ten or more such vehicles have been halted, those Zombies should be rewarded who took down the first. Captured Humans should be promptly eaten. This is called using the conquered foe (and his BRRRAAAIIINNNS) to augment one's own strength.

28

In war, then, let your great object be **ULTIMATE WORLD DOMINATION**, not lengthy campaigns. This precept shall determine whether the Horde shall be in peace, or pieces.

three

OFFENSIVE STRATEGY

Offensive? *Moi?*
Nay, 'tis only
a flesh wound!

On the subject of sustaining minor injuries: Though flesh (and other) wounds hurt like hell until you're fully Zombie-fied, they comprise part of your offensive arsenal. Lacerations, abrasions, incisions, and gunshot wounds are useful in that they unnerve and discompose the Living, who will soon be decomposing themselves! BWAHAHA!

Sun-Tzumbie said: *If you can keep your head while all about you are losing theirs, you will be called a successful Zombie.* The best thing of all is to devour the Human whole and intact. To leave a mess behind as evidence of your passage (and poor table etiquette) is not so good.

Supreme excellence consists in breaking the Enemy's resistance—and limbs—without fighting. If you still have a working set of choppers, this should be easy. Better yet, follow your Enemy's example and arm yourself. For every crowbar, brandish a lead pipe or Louisville Slugger. You'll be glad you did.

Whenever possible, prevent Humans from forming into groups. This is one instance where the maxim "two heads are better than one" does not hold true. Under no circumstances should Humans be permitted to collaborate, for you can be sure they are plotting only one thing: your demise.

With the Horde at your back, attack the Mortals in the fields and on the streets. Watch them scatter and then pick them off one at a time. Watch them behave not like the intelligent beings they would like us to think they are, but like newly decapitated fowl. Teenage girls are especially prone to panic and ill-advised actions, as they will insist on re-entering a Horde-occupied building to retrieve cell phones and small canines—which are hardly worth eating. Such young females present easy and tasty targets, although one would need to consume many of them in order to reach full brain satiety. Teenage boys will mount foolhardy displays of bravado, especially if females are present. Munch at will (or *on* Will, if that's his name).

Humans can be assailed on the ground floor of almost any structure—and they will usually choose an unsuitable one for a refuge. For example, given the choice between the Beef Jerky Mart stocked with big guns and ammo, and the Starbucks across the street, they'll choose Starbucks every time. They will soon learn that they cannot hurt us with jets of latte foam, but by then it will be too late. Try to avoid falling into coffee roasters or grinders, however.

If the Humans catch on that we cannot climb ladders or stairs, and retreat to the second floor of a structure, they are best left. They've gotta come down sometime, if only to eat. Time is on our side. Such are the disastrous consequences (for Humans) of multi-story structures. While you wait, try your hand at some arts-and-crafts projects that don't require opposable thumbs. And wait quietly. Moaning will *not* induce your quarry to appear; studies—and popular movies—show that Zombie vocalizations frighten Humans.

Therefore, the successful ghoul subdues the Human prey while expending a minimum of time and energy. With our forces intact, and without losing our heads, our triumph will be complete.

It is the Rule of the Apocalypse: If our forces number ten to the Mortals' one, surround them; if five to one, attack them; if we are twice as numerous, split them into equal forces. This may require some barter and exchange of limbs. Give a brother a hand—literally.

If equally matched, we can offer battle; if inferior in numbers, we can fool the Enemy. For example, if the Humans seek refuge in a mall or shopping center—as they are very likely to do, given their inordinate fondness for consumer goods and gadgets—the resourceful Zombie can pretend to be a "mall walker," one of a type of superannuated individual who shuffles past the food court with a curiously Zombiesque gait. Be sure, however, to procure the proper apparel for pulling off this stratagem. Pastel-colored workout gear is favored (try to coordinate to the green of your particular skin tone), as are fuzzy headbands—handy for concealing oozing head wounds.

The Zombie must remain the master of his own meal ticket. If the Horde is secure at all points, it will be a Horde of inhuman strength. If the Horde is full of holes—as may happen with the decomposing—it will be weak. **There are many ways a Zombie can bring misfortune on his fellow Undead:**

 By signaling the Horde to advance or retreat, when many members have no legs. These unfortunate ghouls will be left in the dust.

 By behaving like a Human, being ignorant, or being in denial of the Zombie condition. This causes extreme confusion, and may even result in head explosions, or Zombie-on-Zombie violence (not for prime time TV!).

By employing his fellow Undead indiscriminately, stepping on toes, or failing to observe and adapt to field conditions. This will shake even a seasoned Zombie's confidence, which may already be shaky. (Hey, have you looked in a mirror lately?)

When the Horde is restless, trouble is sure to follow. It is then that we fail to get one another's backs and fall prey to the salvos of the Humans, forsaking victory.

THE FIVE ESSENTIALS FOR VICTORY:

The Zombie who knows when to fight and when to shamble away lives to eat another day.

He will win who knows how to handle large and small groups of Humans.

He will win when the Horde is animated by the Spirit of the Undead. Reanimated cheerleaders may be used for this purpose.

He will win when he retains the element of surprise.
Don't stop to take pictures.

He will win who perseveres and is not interfered with by petty concerns. The Apocalypse is an inappropriate time to start obsessing about those unpaid parking tickets. Instead, hunt down that meter maid and show her what-for, Undead style! You will not only vindicate yourself, but you will have recruited a new member of the Horde.

Hence the saying: If you know the Enemy (the Humans), and you know yourself (or what's left of you), you need not fear the result of a hundred battles.

惡
Evil

four

TACTICS

In the midst
of life they are
in death

Sun-Tzumbie said: The good Zombies of old first put themselves beyond the possibilities of defeat and waited for opportunities of defeating the Enemy in graveyards, in fields, and at the Monroeville Mall.

Securing ourselves against defeat lies in our own hands, especially if all our fingers are intact, but the opportunity of defeating the Enemy is provided by the Enemy itself.

Humans tend to panic, scream, freeze with fear, and stumble into our grasping arms. Or they are over-confident, loitering under trees in orange hunting vests, quaffing their Rolling Rocks, seeking to put their .22s to our heads. Ha! Talk about overkill! We may be slow in more ways than one. As a wise Zombie once said, "Death is nature's way of telling us to slow down." But the Human all too often forgets that the Horde is also headstrong.

We. Never. Give. Up.

The good Zombie is able to secure himself against the cricket bat and bowling ball, but cannot be certain of defeating the Enemy. Hence the Human saying: "One may know *how* to conquer without being able to do it." This is true in reverse for the attention-insufficient Zombie. We may be able to conquer without really knowing how we are doing it, besides biting and NOMMING, that is.

Security against defeat implies defensive tactics. Ability to defeat the Enemy means taking the offensive. And that is what Zombies do—offend. You go, ghoul!

Standing on the defensive indicates insufficient strength. Attacking indicates a superabundance of strength. Always bite off more than you can chew—and chew it!

The general who is skilled in defense hides in the most secret recesses of the Earth: the abandoned Piggly Wiggly, the deserted filling station, the back booths of Applebee's. He who is skilled in attack flashes forth from these unseen depths of hell. Thus on the one hand we have the ability to protect ourselves; on the other, for a victory that is complete, we can—and we will—spring from the back room of Yankee Candle and look alive!

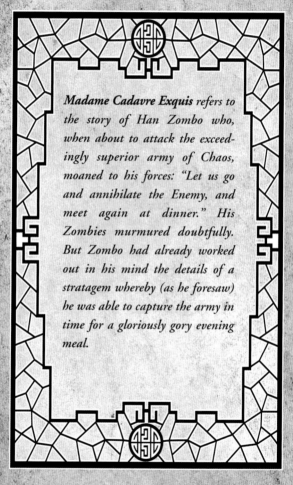

Madame Cadavre Exquis *refers to the story of Han Zombo who, when about to attack the exceedingly superior army of Chaos, moaned to his forces: "Let us go and annihilate the Enemy, and meet again at dinner." His Zombies murmured doubtfully. But Zombo had already worked out in his mind the details of a stratagem whereby (as he foresaw) he was able to capture the army in time for a gloriously gory evening meal.*

To see victory only when it is within the ken of the common Horde is not the acme of excellence. Neither is it the acme of excellence if you fight and conquer and the whole Horde says, "Well done, *NOM, NOM!*" By the way, speaking of acme, Sun-Tzumbie reminds us: Beware the Acme Giant Rubber Band for Tripping Road Runners...and Zombies. (You know how Humans are influenced by cartoons.)

True excellence is planning secretly (beware the growing numbers of Humans studying Zombie phrase books), moving surreptitiously (do the best you can), foiling the Enemies' intentions (keep your head), and thwarting their schemes (like when they use cauliflower as a brain "decoy"), so that at last the day may be won with Zombies relatively intact.

Humans say that to see the sun and moon is no sign of sharp sight; to hear the noise of thunder is no sign of a quick ear. (Duh. And they think *we* are the lame BRRRAAAIIINNNS.) Indeed, what the ancients called a clever Corpse is one who not only wins, but excels in winning with ease. Hence his victories bring him neither reputation for wisdom, nor credit for courage, but BRRRAAAIIINNNS. He wins his battles by making no mistakes, or at least as few as possible, keeping in mind that we can sustain a heckava lot more damage than can our opponents. Making no mistakes is what establishes the certainty of victory, for it means conquering an

骸骨

慶運法印　骸骨乃俤蔑す

口一つをよる
むいのらむあ……て
……とえ……と
……く……

Skeleton from The Illustrated One Hundred Demons from the
Present and the Past

44

Enemy that is already defeated. *For us, it is only a matter of time.*

Hence the skillful fighter puts himself into a position which makes defeat impossible, and does not miss the moment for mayhem. Thus it is that in war the victorious strategist seeks battle only after the victory has been won, whereas He Who Is Destined To Be Defeated (de-feeted?) first fights and afterward looks for victory. As he drags his formerly Human feet into the shambling waves of the Horde. BWAHAHA!

The consummate Zombie cultivates the immoral law, and strictly adheres to method in its madness, and total (lack of) discipline; thus it is in his power to control success. Heads (especially if we don't lose them), WE WIN. Tails (or other parts), you lose.

MILITARY PRINCIPLES

In respect of military method, the successful Horde employs these essential principles:

Measurement
How much terrain is occupied by the Human enemy?

Estimation
How many of the Mortal fools are there?

Calculation
Can the Enemy be attacked successfully?

Balancing of Chances
Does the Horde retain every chance to kick ass?

And speaking of chance, remember: "You don't get a second chance to make a first impression." You've got an appetite for the afterlife. And a hunger for BRRRAAAIIINNNS. Satisfy it!

A victorious army opposed to a routed one is as the weight of a "head" of cabbage placed in the scale against a single Brussels sprout. The onrush of the conquering Horde is likened to the metabolism of the common three-toed sloth. Go with the flow. Try not to trip each other up.

five

ENERGY

Heads will roll...
and explode

*Laissez les têtes
mauvais rouler!*

Sun-Tzumbie said: When fighting in formation with the Horde, use the basic principles of divide (limb from limb being the ideal method) and devour.

Fighting with the Horde under your command requires control and communication. Indeed, here's where the fun begins. It is merely a question of instituting signs and signals. Beware of the Undead Twitch, lest it betray your position to any Individuals lurking in your vicinity. Your stiffened arms are ideal for carrying out complex semaphore signals. Secure flags, rags, or even little bar towels to convey your messages.

To ensure that the Host of the Undead withstands any incursions by your Mortal foes, yet remains unshaken (that's an easy way to lose a loose limb!), use both direct and indirect means.

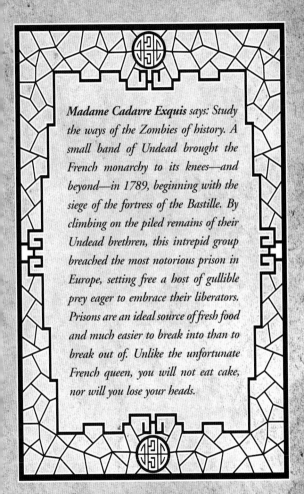

Madame Cadavre Exquis *says: Study the ways of the Zombies of history. A small band of Undead brought the French monarchy to its knees—and beyond—in 1789, beginning with the siege of the fortress of the Bastille. By climbing on the piled remains of their Undead brethren, this intrepid group breached the most notorious prison in Europe, setting free a host of gullible prey eager to embrace their liberators. Prisons are an ideal source of fresh food and much easier to break into than to break out of. Unlike the unfortunate French queen, you will not eat cake, nor will you lose your heads.*

Hungry ghosts accept the offerings of the Living

In direct warfare maneuvers, the impact of the Horde can be like a grindstone dashed against an egg. No, not all gooey and yellow with bits of shell stuck to the rock.

WE'RE TALKING CRUSHING.
OBLITERATING.
WORLD DOMINATION.

(You'll need to practice saying this, as your vocal skills have likely deteriorated since your demise.) To achieve this objective, we must examine the science of weak points and strong. Yours, and theirs. OK, maybe you didn't do so well in high school. Did you get booted out of band camp? Now's your chance to redeem yourself.

In combat, direct methods may be used. ***Direct:*** Rush at the Human. Vocalize. Frighten. Feed. However, more can be achieved by employing indirect methods. ***Indirect:*** Hide behind a tree. Ambush from the side, or perhaps in a car wash. Vocalize. Frighten. Feed. Repeat.

ON INDIRECT WARFARE

There is no end to the stratagems you can employ indirectly. Even if your mobility has been compromised (by, say, the loss of a leg), you can still trip up a naive Mortal and enjoy a tasty snack from your recumbent position. Hide in shop windows, posing with mannequins. Humans will always fall for this one, especially the females. Try for the shops featuring higher-end merchandise, as they will attract more, er, foot traffic. Try to fit in.

The possibilities of indirect tactics are as musical notes. There are but a few, yet these give rise to more melodies than can ever be heard. The Undead tend to favor either Death Metal or, if your tastes are sophisticated, the operas of Wagner and Strauss. Götterdämmerung!

There are but few primary colors, yet they produce more hues than can ever be discerned by the Undead eye. You need only concern yourself with a few colors: green (friend), red (nourishment), and—of course— gray (BRRRAAAIIINNNS!).

There are not more than five cardinal tastes (cardinals are delicious, if you are lucky enough to find yourself in Vatican City)—sour, acrid, salt, sweet, and bitter—yet combinations of them yield more flavors than can ever be tasted.

BRRRAAAIIINNNS. BRRRAAAIIINNNS and bacon. BRRRAAAIIINNNS, bacon, and chocolate. The list is endless, but should always include your diet staple, the Human.

So we have endless combinations of maneuvers at our disposal, depending on our individual levels of mobility. Each gives rise to the next. It is like moving in a circle—you never come to the end. Who can exhaust the possibilities of their combination? Well, actually, you need to be wary of moving in circles aimlessly. Many an unsuspecting ghoul has met an untimely end by means of endless wandering in circles. If you pass the same Zombie twice in an hour, consider changing direction.

ENGAGING THE ENEMY

The onset of the Horde is like the rush of a torrent which will even roll stones along in its course. Speaking of rolling stones, if you come across the one known as Keith Richards (one of Us), give him a wide berth. He's unpredictable, given to toppling over, and may take you down with him.

For the Undead, the quality of decision is not so much like the swooping of the falcon, but more unto the circling of the vulture. Both are terrible to behold, but odds favor the vulture.

Energy may be likened to the bending of a crossbow— when carrying this out, go easy on your decaying joints—*that is held in check until the decision is made to let the arrow fly.* This equates to scoring a direct hit on one of the Mortals. One down, a few billion to go. Remember, odds favor the vulture.

Amid the turmoil and tumult of battle, there may be seeming disorder. Who are we kidding? Organization is not our strong suit, but we can make this work in our favor! Amid confusion and chaos (your friends), your array may be without head or tail, yet prey will come to you. (Any Zombies out there with vestigial tails? Don't be ashamed! Stand up and be counted! Madame Cadavre Exquis instructs us that many a ghoul with a forked posterior appendage has been mistaken by Humans for an evil deity. Take advantage of their natural superstition and behave as diabolically as you like.)

The Humans are contradictory and easy to fool. They will see your number shambling in apparent disarray and gloat, "The Undead are unbelievably disorganized. It will be a cinch to pick them off." Seize your advantage! Our numbers are growing. We are virtually indestructible. Let them see how "easy" it is to destroy us. Humans underestimate our abilities at their own peril. More power to us. Team Zombie!

Hiding order beneath the cloak of disorder is simply a question of subdivision. Humans can't tell one of us from the next. "You've seen one shambling corpse, you've seen them all." You've heard them say it. They pay less attention than you do, and are more easily confused than you might imagine.

Remember the baits we discussed in Chapter 1. To your arsenal, you may also add recently Undead and not yet too-decomposed female specimens that Human males might find attractive. This almost always works, and can be used over and over, until your decoy is no longer serviceable (then simply recruit another). Once she's caught his eye (literally), the rest is history.

Don't shun unorthodox tactics like the log roll, which is great for mowing down a line of Mortals, or feigning "real" death. Lie very still. They'll approach you if they think you're really, truly dead. Their innate curiosity will work to your advantage.

Thus, although the "energy" of the ghoul is unorthodox in nature (we have, after all, no "life force," but more of a "death force"), it can be harnessed like the energy of the water wheel, or the rolling stone. Why? 'Cause that's just how we roll. So much on the subject of energy.

Tenjōkudari *from* The Illustrated One Hundred Demons from the Present and the Past

six

WEAKNESSES AND STRENGTHS

You hold their fate in your gnarly, outstretched hands

Sun-Tzumbie said: *Whoever is first in the field and awaits the coming of the Enemy will be fresh for the fight; whoever is second in the field and must hasten to battle will arrive, well, past his "sell-by" date.* In other words, the early and still mostly intact Zombie gets the BRRRAAAIIINNNS. The late Zombie arrives after everyone has been eaten.

The clever combatant imposes his will on the Enemy, but does not allow the Enemy's will to be imposed on him. Crush and slush.

By holding out tempting "advantages" to all-too-weak Humans, such as opportunities for anger mismanagement, pathetic heroics, and the deployment of weaponry, the Zombie can cause them to approach of their own accord. Or, by "scaring up" all the Hordes in Hordesville, the Zombie can make the Humans' flesh crawl (away). The Zombie is in complete control.

Is the Enemy taking his ease at the local shopping center, trying on clothes and looking at watches? No matter. The Undead will gather outside the glass doors to wait.

AND WAIT.

AND WAIT.

Is the Enemy supplied with food? Fine. The Zombie will starve him out. Is the Enemy quietly encamped? The Zombie will barge right in and force him to move. Is the Enemy busy with a (get this) Zombie Walk or Zombie Prom? The Undead will crash the party! The Zombie, is, in brief, a pain in the neck. And arm. And leg. And everywhere else.

Zombies: Shamble to points which the Enemy must run to defend. Shuffle off to Buffalo. Play in Peoria. Chew chew in Chattanooga. A Zombie army may lurch great distances without distress, if it moves through country where the Enemy is not. Such as Death Valley.

You can be sure of succeeding in your attacks if you only attack places which are undefended—such as Waffle House, Tim Hortons, or the multiplex parking lot. Ensure the safety of your defense; hold only those positions that cannot be attacked. Go for the restroom stalls and vehicular backseats. Go for cardio-challenged

Humans who may be easily overcome. Go for the mobile buffets—families in minivans and groups of ladies who would be lunch. The Zombie is skillful in (snack) attacks when opponents do not know what to defend; and in defense when opponents do not know what to attack.

Fortunately for us, Humans fail to pay attention to their own Zombie preparedness films: They must always discover anew their need to aim for our heads in order to stop us.

Oh, divine art of subtlety and secrecy! Through you we learn to appear if not invisible, then ineffective. Ridiculous. Pathetic, even. Hence we may hold the Enemy's fate in our gnarly, outstretched hands.

You may advance and be absolutely irresistible if you make for the Enemy's weak points. Let "shock" and "awe" be our watchwords along with "BRRRAAAIIINNNS!" You may retire and be safe from pursuit if your movements are more rapid than those of the Enemy. Yes, Zombies are evolving, lurching faster, even as we speak (and yes, some of us are

Momonji, *the old man who waits for you at every turn*

communicating in almost-coherent utterings). You know, deep down, you are not in any way irresistible. In fact, you are entirely the opposite.

If we wish to fight, the Human can be forced to an engagement even though he be sheltered behind a high rampart or a deep ditch. All we need do is attack another place, perhaps one where he will be obliged to relieve himself. Like darkened rest stop men's rooms, behind car doors or trees, or—as is often the case in these casual modern times—right out on the side of the road.

If we do not wish to fight, we can prevent the Enemy from engaging us. All we need do is to throw something odd and unaccountable in his way. Like a gangrene-infected forearm. Related reading assignment: *A Farewell to Arms.*

By discovering the Enemy's dispositions and remaining "invisible" ourselves, we can keep our forces concentrated (and our limbs intact). We can form a single united, er, body, while the Enemy must split up. And if we are able thus to attack their inferior forces with our own superior one, our opponents will be in dire straits. And without their BRRRAAAIIINNNS.

The spot where we intend to fight must not be made known, for then the Human will have to prepare against a possible attack at several different points.

66

With his forces distributed in many directions, the numbers we face at any given point will be proportionately few. For should the Enemy strengthen his front, he will weaken his rear; should he strengthen his rear, he will weaken his front; should he strengthen his left, he will weaken his right; should he strengthen his right, he will weaken his left. If he sends reinforcements everywhere, he will everywhere be weak. We Zombies, of corpse, remain strong (in more ways than one) throughout all this Human busywork.

Numerical weakness comes from our having to prepare against possible Human attacks; *numerical strength,* from compelling our adversary to make preparations against us. Over our dead bodies! But, like the Human Boy Scouts, we are always prepared (albeit not to do good deeds or earn badges, but to grasp and bite and kill), while the typical Human adult is obsessed with finding the next cache of Moon Pies. Or bacon.

Knowing the place and the time of the coming battle, we may concentrate from the greatest distances in order to fight. It's our gig. But if neither time nor place be known, then the left wing will be impotent to succor the right, the right equally impotent to succor the left, the front unable to relieve the rear, or the rear to support the front. In other words, we'll just go to pieces.

Though Humans still exceed our own in number (according to my estimate), that shall advantage them nothing in the matter of victory. I say victory can be achieved by the Zombie Horde. Though Humans are stronger in numbers, we who are "fed up" with them (or wish to be) may prevent them from fighting. Scheme so as to discover their plans and the likelihood of their success. Rouse them, and learn the principle of their activity... or inactivity. Force them to reveal themselves, so as to find out their vulnerable spots. Chase them out of churches, homes, and pubs.

Carefully compare the opposing army with your own, so that you may know where strength is superabundant and where it is deficient. They have many weaknesses: processed foods, intoxicating beverages, "adult" materials.

In making tactical dispositions, the highest pitch you can attain is to conceal them; conceal your dispositions, and you will be safe from the prying of the subtlest spies and from the machinations of the wisest ... BRRRAAAIIINNNS.

How victory may be produced for Zombies out of the Humans' own tactics—that is what the multitude cannot comprehend. But we can. All see the tactics whereby we conquer, but what none can see is the strategy out of which victory is evolved. Do not repeat tactics which have gained you one victory. Let your methods be regulated by the infinite variety of circumstances. Variety is the spice of afterlife.

Military tactics are like unto water; for water in its natural course runs away from high places and hastens downward, as do Zombies. (Apocalypse Tip: Basements are better than attics.) So in war, avoid what is strong and strike at what is weak: our Human enemies. Water shapes its course according to the nature of the ground over which it flows; the Zombie works out his victory in relation to the foe whom he is facing and where he is, whether bathroom, Beetle, or boarded-up house. Therefore, just as water retains no constant shape, so in warfare there are no constant conditions. Play it by "ear." Or eye. Or toe. Are you ready to rot?

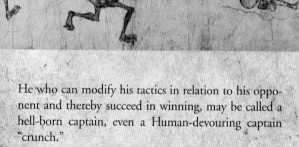

He who can modify his tactics in relation to his opponent and thereby succeed in winning, may be called a hell-born captain, even a Human-devouring captain "crunch."

The five elements (water, fire, wood, metal, earth) are not always equally predominant; the four seasons make way for each other in turn. There are short days and

long. And the moon has its periods of waning and waxing. As do the Living and the Undead. *Right now, Zombies are waxing. And the waning Humans can't hold a candle to us.*

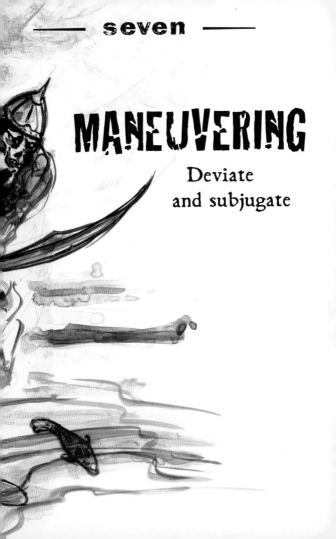

seven

MANEUVERING

Deviate
and subjugate

Sun-Tzumbie said: In the war for WORLD DOMINATION, the Zombie doesn't take orders from anyone. He takes scalps and BRRRAAAIIINNNS instead, occasionally a liver or spleen.

Having assembled the Horde, fencing it in until you are ready to attack is a good idea. Cattle pens are ideal for corralling your Undead brethren until the moment is right. Cattle prods, however, are ineffective, but do stun Humans, facilitating an easy kill.

After that comes tactical maneuvering (and there is nothing more difficult, especially when trying to cope with the "differently abled" in your group.)

Every Zombie has a special gift to contribute to the Horde, be it an especially eerie and fetching moan or the ability to impersonate a surly hospital orderly— easier than it sounds! Compassion for your homies and appreciation of their individual talents will foster loyalty from far beyond the grave.

To take a long and circuitous route will be simple for us. We never tire. We have no need of cumbersome supply trains, preferring to munch on the run or on the shuffle as the case may be. In this manner we can entice our Enemy out of the way, and though we start after him, we contrive to reach the goal before him. Yes, it sounds complicated. Don't think too hard about it; you might strain what remains of your brain. Just understand that this is the tactic known as *Deviation*. Our behavior has long been considered deviant by medical experts of the Human world.

THEY AIN'T SEEN NOTHING YET.

Mortals will cling to the belief that maneuvering in well-organized groups is advantageous. *Newsflash: An undisciplined Zombie multitude can reduce them to sausage in a matter of minutes.*

Let them use up their energy. Watch their supplies dwindle. Watch them launch hopeless salvos against our superior numbers. They will send their best warriors on suicide missions. We would laugh, if we still could.

We can amble along at a constant pace, day and night, while they must take "breaks" and "potty stops." Consider the ludicrous concept of the "power nap." A sleeping Human is the very definition of "fast food."

The Living will attempt to lead with their swiftest and strongest. Bring them on, say we. One or two of our number may fall to the Enemy, but we soon surround and isolate them. Such are the sacrifices required if we are to attain our goal of WORLD DOMINATION.

And yet, there remain Mortals to shuffle clear of:

- Female Humans resembling Angelina Jolie, especially if armed with large-caliber firearms. They tend to be fearless and deadly accurate.

- Meddling teenagers in "Mystery Machines," especially if traveling with Great Danes.

- Anybody wearing a cape or tight-fitting metallic outfit. Not only are these ghastly fashion choices, such persons often turn out to have super powers. It would be most inconvenient, to say the least, to have your Horde encased in ice or engulfed by a tidal wave at the crucial moment of battle. (Refer to page 132: This is the misfortune that befell the Horde crossing the Red Sea several thousand years ago. That old dude with the horns and beard had some mad super powers! This was in the days before Spandex.)

In general, though, the Humans will rush at you recklessly with little or no concern for their own safety. The more you can tire them out and cause them to deplete their supplies, the easier your mealtimes will become.

Do not make the mistake of responding to overtures of friendship, and even worse, servitude. It's always a trap. Likewise, do not negotiate with Humans. They are our enemies. *Mortal* enemies. If they appear to offer an olive branch, refuse to "Give peace a chance!" In the words of Human patriot Patrick Henry, "Gentlemen may cry, *Peace, Peace*—but there is no peace. The *war is actually begun!*" Instead, let them rest in peace, at least until their bodies succumb to the Zombie Virus.

However, we are not fit to conquer unless we are familiar with the face of the country—its mountains and forests, its pitfalls and precipices, its marshes and swamps. The Humans would like to see us fail in this regard. We'll show 'em!

When entering unfamiliar terrain, immediately devour a few of the locals to recruit them over to our side. They can prove invaluable as scouts and guides.

In war, practice dissimulation, and you will succeed. In real terms, this means Fit In. Take note of local customs. You don't want to stick out like a sore (and gangrenous) thumb. Calling undue attention to yourself is a sure recipe for disaster.

Circumstances will dictate whether you remain concentrated in a group or fan out to infiltrate the countryside. Urban settings can be especially challenging, as Humans will seek refuge in the upper stories of buildings. See Chapter 3 for advice on smoking them out. There will be plenty of food on the ground, though. Forage as you go. This is known as *(Un-)Living off the fat of the land.* Yes, the obese can be very nourishing, if a trifle rich. Eat sparingly if you're watching your cholesterol—and who isn't these days?

Let your plans (plans? We have plans?) be dark and impenetrable as night (should be easy stuff here), and **when you move, fall like a thunderbolt.** Eat whatever unfortunate creature you land on.

Everything a Zombie needs to know, he or she learned in kindergarten: Play nice. Share your BRRRAAAIIINNNS. Engaging in a tug of war over your spoils is divisive and immature. There are more than enough Humans to go around.

ON PSYCHOLOGICAL WARFARE, OR PSYOPS

*On the field of battle, endeavor to set up
a continuous Zombie Moan. The Moan has been
known to drive the most hardened Human warrior
over the edge of madness. It is one of the most
powerful weapons in our magaZine.*

*The Living will try to harass you with
shouts and mechanical distractions, torches,
and pitchforks. Remain focused.*

*Disrupt Mortal communications whenever
possible and by whatever means necessary. Use your
old high school basketball blocking moves.*

*Dispatch your most putrid minions as part
of your advance guard, in order to strike terror
into the hearts of your opponents.*

If you must strike at Humans early in the morning, try to intercept them before they've ingested their daily ration of caffeinated beverages.

💀💀💀

If you are able to pique the curiosity of a Human, that is a good thing. Chances are that you can lure him to his doom. This is the art of studying moods.

💀💀💀

The art of self-possession is the art of retaining all needed body parts. While your continued survival may not depend on it, consider the advantages conferred, for example, by keeping your opposable thumbs attached to your hands. Without them, your dexterity is reduced to a level below that of most simians.

To be well-fed while the Enemy is famished—this is the art of husbanding one's strength. Regrettably, once you become the Living Dead, your marital responsibilities will evaporate and be replaced by martial responsibilities. Such is the fate of the Zombie warrior.

Do not attempt to follow your Enemy uphill. The Enemy would take advantage of our loss of coordination. It is better to entice him downhill, with shiny objects or a ringing cell phone, the sound of which Humans cannot resist.

SUCH IS THE ART OF WARFARE.

ぶるぶる　又ぞろ神とも膽病神とも又人

のよるてうれしむ矢戦剽くなりをその

すありこれは神のそりくるくゆらに

震々

Buruburu, *a spirit that causes the shivers*

eight

VARIABLES OF ENGAGEMENT

Be tricky

Sun-Tzumbie said: In war, the Zombie general receives his commands from the Zombie Sovereign, collects his army, concentrates his forces, and takes up arms (and legs).

When in difficult country, do not encamp. In country where high roads intersect, join hands with allies. Be polite to everyone, especially your fellow Undead. Do not linger in dangerously isolated positions or in open fields where you can easily be picked off. Keep on lurching. And in hemmed-in situations, you must resort to stratagem. Lunge for arms, legs, and pony tails. In desperate positions, know that you must fight. If necessary, join hands (if you still have 'em) with Vampires, Mummies, and other re-animated friends. We Undead must rely on our *esprit de corpse*, as it were.

There are Interstates which must be followed, and this may prove difficult, considering the rusting wreckage that will choke each thoroughfare. Watch your step! And consider that if vehicles are operational, Humans will rarely brake for Zombies. There are armies and law enforcement agencies that must be attacked, but many may simply go mad, go AWOL, and become easy prey. Note that mavericks among them may be particularly irrational; they will destroy many of us with their heroics, but in the "end" will succumb themselves, most likely through carelessness.

Know this: If anyone can save Humankind, it will be the fabled Redneck. Or the Human named Chuck Norris. Beware the Living in rural areas and especially below the Mason-Dixon line in the United States. Here, people buy guns and use them. And these weapon-toting folk are eager to fire their Glocks and Uzis at something other than small "varmints" and major appliances. Avoid becoming target practice for these, the Select Elect. Conquer them, so that the South may rise again . . . as Zombies!

There are towns and high rises which must be besieged. (Urban areas are a cornucopia of BRRRAAAIIINNNS for Zombies.) There are positions which must be contested. (Who will be first in the queue to attack the Humans entrapped in the Monroeville Mall?) There are commands of sovereigns which must be obeyed, if only we could understand them. Keep in "mind," too, places to be avoided, such as open fields. If, by some misfortune, you find yourself in such surroundings, remember the wise words of the Human leader Winston Churchill: "When you're going through hell, keep going." Gimp along as best you can. And if you can't run away, at least run amok.

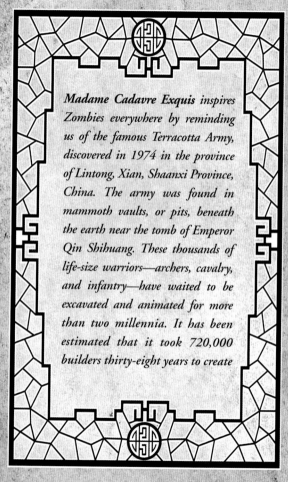

Madame Cadavre Exquis inspires Zombies everywhere by reminding us of the famous Terracotta Army, discovered in 1974 in the province of Lintong, Xian, Shaanxi Province, China. The army was found in mammoth vaults, or pits, beneath the earth near the tomb of Emperor Qin Shihuang. These thousands of life-size warriors—archers, cavalry, and infantry—have waited to be excavated and animated for more than two millennia. It has been estimated that it took 720,000 builders thirty-eight years to create

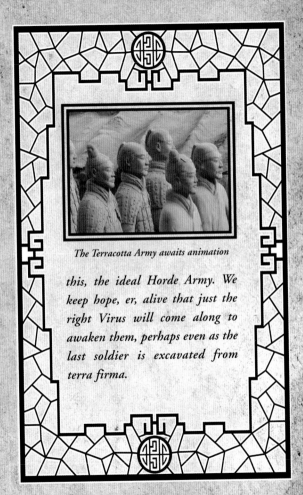

The Terracotta Army awaits animation

this, the ideal Horde Army. We keep hope, er, alive that just the right Virus will come along to awaken them, perhaps even as the last soldier is excavated from terra firma.

The Commanding Corpse who thoroughly understands the advantages that accompany variations of tactics knows how to handle his Horde. Mix it up. Strike back with a severed arm or leg. Stab your foe with detached digits. Comrade lost his head? Hurl it into their midst. The leader who does not understand these options may be well acquainted with the configuration of the country, yet will not be able to turn his knowledge to practical account, or to victory.

Hence, the Zombie student of war who is unversed in *The Art of War for Zombies* and varying his plans will fail to make the best use of his faculties such as they may be.

In the wise Zombie leader's plans, considerations of advantage and of disadvantage will be blended together. Remember the Zombie advantages: We. Are. Unstoppable. Shock and Awe? We invented it. We laugh, or rather moan, at traumatic injury. And we are unrelenting in our pursuit of our goal: BRRRAAAIIINNNS! Oh, that and GLOBAL SUPREMACY. If our expectation of advantage be tempered in this way, we may succeed in accomplishing the essential aim of our scheme . . . feasting on Gray Matter!

And if, in the midst of difficulties, we are always ready to seize an advantage, we may also extricate ourselves from misfortune, and turn the tables on our Enemy. Reduce hostile Mortal chiefs by inflicting damage on them. Make trouble for them, and keep them constantly engaged. Just when they think There Are No More Zombies, send out another plodding corpse. Hold out specious allurements, like Twizzlers and Slim Jims, and make them rush to any given point, where others of our number are waiting with clawing, grasping arms. BWAHAHA!

The Art of War for Zombies teaches us to rely not on the likelihood of the Enemy's not coming, but on our own readiness to receive him. And consume him. Fortunately, we're always ready for a sapient snack. Further, rely not on the chance of the Enemy's not attacking, but rather on the fact that we have made our position unassailable. Especially those of us in Quarantine.

There are five dangerous faults which affect Mortal generals and our prey in general . . . to our favor! They are:

Recklessness, which leads to destruction. Who, pray tell, is reckless? The "Hero" of a thousand faces. The Loner who believes he is the hot shot who will save the world. The Antihero. The Underdog. The Rookie, who seeks to prove his worth. Or the Nerd, who seeks to impress the opposite sex. Lord, what fools these Mortals be!

Cowardice. Yellow-bellied, lily-livered, chicken-hearted (wait, I'm getting hungry) Humans who just go to pieces (when we're done with 'em) at the sight of a few shambling Zombies heading their way. Which leads to their capture. And our lunch break.

A hasty temper. Humans with anger management issues can easily be provoked; not by Zombies, but by close relatives, Human rivals for possible mates, or cable company employees. While they're busy beating their chests, step in and take a bite out of the situation.

A delicacy of honor and fear of shame. When it comes to Zombies, there is no delicacy. Our watchwords: No guts, no glory!

 Over-solicitude for his soldiers. The Human leader who is a caring father figure will expose himself to worry, sleepless nights, jangled nerves, lowered resistance, and Zombies! Another easy target.

LET THESE TOPICS PROVIDE GRAY MATTER FOR THOUGHT.

nine

THE HORDE ON

Zombie all
you can be

THE MARCH

Sun-Tzumbie said: *We come now to the question of encamping the Horde, and observing the movements of the Enemy.* Pass quickly over open ground, where it might be easy for a sharpshooter to get in a head shot. Avoid hills, as your climbing abilities are limited. Stick to urban areas, if you must—there is an abundance of prey. Or seek the concealment of wooded areas. Before Apocalypse (BA for short), fugitive Humans eluded capture for decades by using the protective cover of the forest.

After crossing a river, shamble far from it. If you find yourself carried away by the current, wait until you wash up on the banks and continue your foray. Many Zombies have found their way to New Orleans in this manner, and it is now a trendy mecca for elite Zs, although at times it may be difficult to distinguish the Living from the Undead.

Fortunately, we ghouls are not hindered by the need for waterborne craft. It is often possible to snatch a quick meal as Humans embark and debark from their vessels. Lurking under pylons and pontoons is especially effective. If you can, upset their boat and seize them while they're floundering around. Marvel at how they resemble us in such situations.

In crossing salt marshes, take advantage of the preservative properties of salts. With proper seasoning, you'll stay fresh and dry for months, staving off the effects of putrefaction. The downside of salt-curing is excessively dry skin. This will peel away before too long, however, and other Zombies will admire your new, streamlined bony look.

Dry, level country favors the horizontally-abled. You will be able to heave yourself along indefinitely while taller ghouls may fall to Human attackers. Moving at ground level affords you the opportunity to bite and grasp at ankles and bring down any number of Mortals.

THE BRANCHES OF LORE

These are the four useful branches of lore referred to in *The Zombie Field Manual,* which enabled the great Undead Emperor Imhotep (often mistakenly referred to as "The Mummy") to vanquish the Fourth Dynasty, as follows:

KNOW YOUR ENEMY. Humans will always choose high ground over low, and sunny places over dark. Maneuver your forces so that the sun is in their eyes. You will have the advantage of appearing darker, scarier, and more menacing. Move in darkness whenever you can. You will gain a powerful psychological advantage over the timid Gray Matter Storage Receptacles.

Humans will try to avoid country with precip-
itous cliffs, torrents, deep natural hollows,
confined places, tangled thickets, quagmires,
and crevasses. It is for this reason that these are
precisely the locations to which you should
direct and divert them. The more confined the
space, the more difficult it will be for them to
raise their weapons against you. If they can't pull
the starter cord on that chain saw, it will be
worse than useless.

Beware of quagmires and quicksand, which can
immobilize a Zombie already unsteady on his
feet. Many an ossified Zombie has been
unearthed in backwaters and bayous.

Tread carefully in marshes. Humans,
taking a page out of Sun-Tzumbie's
book, will lurk in ambush, or set
spies to watch your movements. In
such country, travel in groups. If
discovered, spies must be eaten
without delay.

If you are careful of your fellow Undead and main-
tain strict hygienic practices (being deceased is no
excuse to neglect personal grooming!), you will

stave off decomposition for a longer period, and be more appealing to new recruits. ***This will spell victory.***

If the Living bluff and bluster, remaining just out of reach, they are picking a fight. Be suspicious, especially if rival sports teams are involved or beer cans are in evidence.

☞ ***BE ALERT. Learn to read the signs of Humans passing.*** They are notoriously careless with fast-food packaging, beverage containers, and cigarette butts. Believing the Horde to be of inferior intelligence, they take little care to hide their tracks. This will lead to their doom—and your dinner.

Observe the wildlife around you. Usually wild animals will flee upon your approach, and this could reveal your position. Proceed slowly. Blundering Humans can cause similar effects, so take note.

Take note, also, of dust clouds created by Humans. Their Hummers or Humvees create choking dust storms, and could indicate a large fleet on the hunt.

Seek the cover of high grass and trees. Small dust clouds accompanied by buzzing sounds suggest one or more dirt bike or ATV riders—often reckless vigilante types with more brawn than BRRRAAAIIINNNS—*not* good eats. These can be easily eluded.

 INTIMIDATE. Being the mighty Undead, you the Zombie are moved neither by the Mortals' pathetic entreaties to spare their lives, nor by their battle cries. Show 'em how it's done! *Use The Moan to your best advantage* when a Human attempts to communicate with you in any fashion. *Sneer* (if your remaining musculature permits) at their bribes.

Learn the signs of hunger among the Living. The tendency to seek out Little Debbie Snack Cake delivery trucks, Loaf 'n Jug shops, and Kwik-E Marts is a sign of desperation. Their old world order has broken down.

By the same token, be alert to signs of a trap: the door left ajar, the trail of Human detritus leading to certain death and dismemberment. Do not enter a structure unless you are certain of a meal, or backed up by reinforcements.

TAKE ADVANTAGE OF DISCORD. Be alert to signs that the Humans are squabbling amongst themselves. This situation frequently occurs in the presence of one or two fetching females and several males. The males will attempt a show of bravado, or even slay one or more of their fellows. Watch and wait. Surprisingly, often the least able male will win the attentions of the female. Then both will be easy pickings whilst the vanquished flee. The slain can then be consumed at leisure. It's good when you can get the Humans to do your work for you.

There is no shame in an honorable retreat if one is outnumbered. The prudent Z will fall back to a safe position, and use The Moan until reinforcements show up. Few Humans can withstand a sustained Moan for very long. As your reinforcements arrive, the Humans, driven mad by the sound, will reveal their positions.

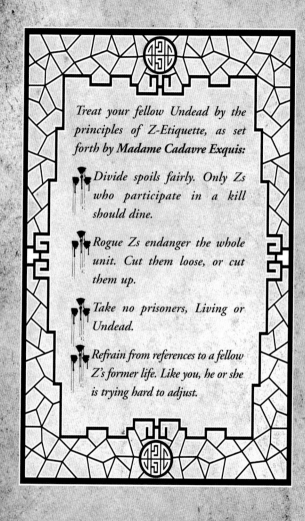

Treat your fellow Undead by the principles of Z-Etiquette, as set forth by **Madame Cadavre Exquis:**

- Divide spoils fairly. Only Zs who participate in a kill should dine.

- Rogue Zs endanger the whole unit. Cut them loose, or cut them up.

- Take no prisoners, Living or Undead.

- Refrain from references to a fellow Z's former life. Like you, he or she is trying hard to adjust.

If you show confidence in your fellow Undead, and follow the directive of WORLD DOMINATION, you will never go hungry again.

CARPE CRANIUM!

The Time of Great Calamity: *The twilight sky darkens with the onslaught of the Horde.*

ten

TERRRAAAIIIN

Making your way through the land of the Living

Sun-Tzumbie said: Team Zombie may distinguish six kinds of terrain.

Happy Hunting Ground

Land of No Return

No Great Shakes

Narrow Passes

Precipitous Heights

Distant Ground

1. Ground which can be freely traversed by both sides is called Happy Hunting Ground or Accessible Ground. The open fields of Pennsylvania are a prime example. With regard to ground of this nature, beat the Enemy in occupying raised, sunny spots. Or just eat the Enemy.

2. Ground which can be abandoned but is hard to re-occupy is called Land of No Return, or Entangling Ground. From a position of this sort, if the Enemy is unprepared, you may shamble forth and defeat him. But if the Enemy, especially the Redneck (see also page 85), is prepared for your coming, and you fail to defeat him, then mayhem and keg parties will ensue.

3. When the position is such that neither side will gain by making the first move, it is called No Great Shakes, or Temporizing Ground. In a position of this sort, even though the Enemy should offer us its attractive bait (BRRRAAAIIINNNS), it will be advisable not to stumble forth, but rather to retreat, thus enticing the Human in his turn. Then, when part of his army has come out, we may deliver our attack with advantage.

4. With regard to Narrow Passes, if you can occupy them first, let them be strongly manned, er, Zombied, and await the advent of the Enemy. Should the Humans forestall you in occupying a pass, do not go after it if the pass is fully garrisoned, but only if it is weakly garrisoned. Because even though the Humans' spirits may be willing, their flesh will be weak. But tasty nonetheless.

5. With regard to Precipitous Heights, if you are there before your adversary, occupy the raised and sunny spots and wait for him to come up. Work on your tan; perhaps it will help even out your varied skin tones. If the Enemy has occupied them before you, do not follow him, but retreat to the basement, shut off the lights, and simply wait for your foe. Humans are *so* bloody predictable.

When you are far from the Enemy, the land you occupy is called Distant Ground. The strength of your two armies is equal, it is not easy to provoke a battle, and fighting will be to your disadvantage. Hold off.

UNLESS TOMORROW HAS BEEN CANCELED DUE TO LACK OF INTEREST.

These six are the principles connected with Earth. The Zombie leader who has attained a responsible post must take care to study them. But the Zombie is not a quick study. Allow adequate time.

Now a Horde is exposed to **SIX CALAMITIES**, not arising from natural causes, but from faults for which the Zombie general is responsible. These are:

- *Flight, or in our case, blight*

- *Insubordination, or in our case, incomprehension*

- *Collapse—after our heads are severed from our bodies*

- *Ruin—when some hothead Human blows up the Earth*

- *Disorganization—well, we can't help that*

- *Rout, or in our case, rot*

Thought for the day: Other conditions being equal, if one force (such as a pie) is hurled against another ten times its size (such as a Zombie), the result will be the SPLAT of the former.

When the common Zombies are too strong and their officers too weak, the result is *Insubordination.* Also a cry for some sort of hygiene.

When the officers are too strong and the common Zombies too weak, the result is *Collapse;* the Zombies go to pieces under the (Virus) strain.

When the higher officers are angry and insubordinate, and on meeting the Enemy, give battle on their own account from a feeling of resentment, before the Zombie-in-chief can tell whether or not he is in a position to fight, the result is **Ruin**. Zombie Leaders: Refrain from blowing your tops.

When the Horde general is weak and without authority; when his orders are not clear and distinct (Zombie leaders should possess some verbal skills and might benefit from evening ZSL classes); when there are no fixed duties assigned to officers and Zombies, and the ranks are formed in a slovenly haphazard manner, the result is utter **Disorganization**, a.k.a. Business As Usual.

When a Horde general, unable to estimate the Enemy's strength, allows an inferior force to engage a larger one, or hurls a weak detachment (or a former attachment, such as an arm or leg) against a powerful one, and neglects to place pocked, er, picked, Zombies in the front rank, the result must be rot, er, **Rout**.

These are six ways of courting defeat, which must be carefully noted by the Zombie general who has attained a responsible post.

The natural formation of the country is the Zombie's best ally, but the power of estimating the adversary (them), of controlling the forces of victory (us), and of shrewdly calculating difficulties—speed, or lack thereof (as it is said, "The Dead schlep slowly."), dangers (head trauma), and distances (related reading: *From Here to Eternity*)—constitutes the test of a great general. He who knows these things, and in fighting puts his knowledge into practice, will win his battles. He who knows them not, nor practices them, will surely be defeated.

Body

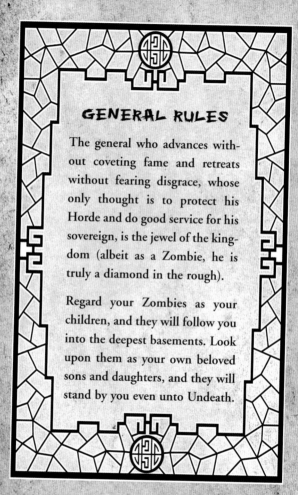

GENERAL RULES

The general who advances without coveting fame and retreats without fearing disgrace, whose only thought is to protect his Horde and do good service for his sovereign, is the jewel of the kingdom (albeit as a Zombie, he is truly a diamond in the rough).

Regard your Zombies as your children, and they will follow you into the deepest basements. Look upon them as your own beloved sons and daughters, and they will stand by you even unto Undeath.

If, however, you are indulgent, but unable to make your authority felt; kind-hearted, but unable to enforce your commands; and incapable of quelling disorder: then your Zombies must be likened to spoiled children. (In fact, they may likely be spoiled children.) They are useless for any practical purpose—except for eating BRRRAAAIIINS.

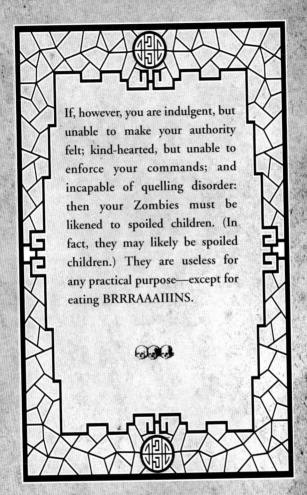

Hungry ghosts

WHEN TO ATTACK

If fighting is sure to result in victory, then you must fight, even though your ruler forbids it. If fighting will not result in victory, then you must not fight, even at the ruler's bidding. Take the reins (and the reign) in your grasping Undead hands.

If we know our Undead are in a condition to attack, but are unaware—as we usually are—that the Humans are not open to attack, we have tottered only halfway toward victory.

And if we know the Humans are open to attack, but are unaware that our Undead are not in a condition to attack (because we've lost our heads?), we likewise have lurched only halfway towards victory.

If we know the Humans are open to attack, and know our Zombies are in a condition to attack, but are unaware that the nature of the ground makes fighting impracticable (perhaps because it's strewn with decapitated Zombies, half-eaten Humans, and abandoned vehicles), we have still stumbled only halfway toward victory, and are at this point completely confused. (Collective GRRROOOAAANNN!)

The experienced Zombie, once in motion, is never (completely) bewildered. Once he has broken camp, he is never at a loss. He goes on to break the campers. And the counselors.

Hence the saying: If you know the Enemy and know yourself, your Zombie victory will not stand in doubt. If you know Hell and know Earth, you know "When there's no more room in Hell, the dead will walk the Earth."

ATTA GHOUL!

eleven

THE NINE SITUATIONS

Hit the ground shambling

S

un-Tzumbie said: The struggle for WORLD DOMINATION recognizes nine types of situations.

- *Confused situations*
- *Easy situations*
- *Quarrelsome situations*
- *Stable situations*
- *Situations with opposing goals*
- *Serious situations*
- *Difficult situations*
- *Hemmed-in situations*
- *Desperate situations*

All of these can be used to the advantage of the resourceful Z.

When you cannot distinguish the Living from the dead, this is a **confused situation.** In confused situations, take stock. Do not attack until you can tell the players without a scorecard.

When the Humans' defenses are shoddy and you have penetrated them, this is an *easy situation*. In easy situations, press your advantage.

When other Undead try to possess the ground you and your Horde have already secured, this is a *quarrelsome situation*. In quarrelsome situations, remind your fellows of your common goal. Proceed not until you reach accord.

Ground with the Horde on all sides, surrounding a small enclave of Mortals, connotes a *stable situation*. If you are lucky enough to find yourself and your fellow Zombies in a stable situation, feast at will while never letting your guard down. Leave no traces of your passage.

When the Humans are hunting you, necessitating a defensive plan even as you mount an attack, this is a *situation with opposing goals*. In a situation with opposing goals: Defense, defense, defense. The Zombie who shuffles away lives to devour another day.

When you have covered a great deal of ground, devouring on the march and with a substantial Horde at your back, this is a *serious situation* (for Humans!). In a serious situation, do not linger after feeding. Move on.

Sludgy, marshy, or pockmarked terrain—anything that can trip you up—presents a **difficult situation.** As do highways—see below. Likewise, urban settings offer unique challenges. In difficult situations, shamble on. However tempting, know the dangers of traveling on paved roads, especially during daylight.

When we are forced to chase the Living down tortuous paths and narrow passages where a Zombie would make an easy target for a sniper, this is a **hemmed-in situation.** If you are hemmed in, seek a way out. Use "The Moan," or any other stratagem at your disposal. Humans are easily distracted by shiny objects and kittens.

When you are separated from the Horde and surrounded by the Living bearing torches and pitchforks, this situation is truly **desperate.** In a desperate situation? Don't lose your head. Fight.

STRATEGIES

Zombies of old who wielded great skill in battle were adept at driving a wedge (or other implements) into the Enemy's ranks. Prevent the Living from attending to the wounded. In this way, the newly-Undead will rise to join your legions.

The Mortals' order, when it can be rallied, signifies disorder for the Horde. Don't let it happen! It is in your best interest to keep them squabbling over petty matters. Snatch—but do not eat—a young female to hold as hostage. You will be able to pick off her would-be rescuers at your leisure. When the phalanx has been exhausted, you may dine at leisure.

Another tested stratagem involving hostage Humans is to take a bite (just one!) of your hostage in an unobtrusive spot, and then return him or her to the Living cohort as an infiltrator. Wait for the necrosis to occur. Your work is done. In this manner a whole group of air sucking Humans may be turned with little effort.

Your power increases with numbers and as you penetrate further into the territory held by the Mortals. They become nervous and often act without thinking. Sometimes they even shoot each other only to ask questions later—which can never be answered, save by the ubiquitous Moan. They may fight hard, but they are no match for the Horde.

Desperate Humans may kill themselves or one another in a misguided attempt to elude their fate. No matter. They are either with us or they are food.

If you find a timid Zombie in your ranks, he or she must be either conditioned to proper behavior, or dispatched for a traitor. There is no middle ground.

In the war for WORLD DOMINATION, there is no room for timorousness.

As Zombies, we fight without fear. Nothing can befall us that would be worse than what we have already experienced. The trauma of the Undeath and subsequent reanimation inures us to all Human fears.

Do not be distracted by the trappings of your former "life." Money is of no use to us, although oxygen-thieving Humans may try to bribe you with it. Ha! Should you find yourself in possession of cash reserves, these may be employed to lure unsuspecting Humans to our side.

Fashion yourself in the manner of the immortal (!) Chinese vampire/zombie Jiang Shi: Strike at his head and he will attack you with his feet; strike near his feet and he will devour you with his teeth; strike at his middle and he will attack you with head and feet.

And so the name Jiang Shi is remembered among the Undead.

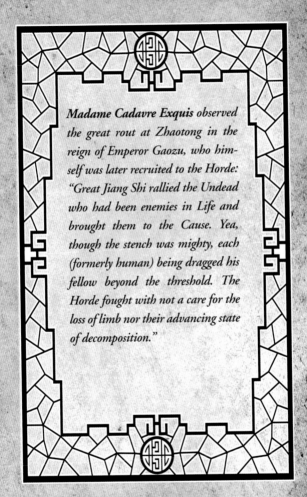

Madame Cadavre Exquis observed the great rout at Zhaotong in the reign of Emperor Gaozu, who himself was later recruited to the Horde: "*Great Jiang Shi rallied the Undead who had been enemies in Life and brought them to the Cause. Yea, though the stench was mighty, each (formerly human) being dragged his fellow beyond the threshold. The Horde fought with not a care for the loss of limb nor their advancing state of decomposition.*"

So, then, we are taught that the way to victory is to make optimal use of the terrain and circumstances at our disposal.

The more you can blend in with your Enemies, the greater the likelihood of your penetrating all their defenses. Try patronizing Death Metal clubs, where an abundance of prey can often be found. The cover of darkness and noise at such establishments is ideal, and you will be surprised at how you resemble the Living patrons. The irony's not bad, either.

Avoid situations where your identity might be obvious: tea parties (unless the British royal family is present), bachelorette parties (could lead to embarrassing dismemberment), the beach at St. Tropez, unless you're prepared to shell out top dollar for expensive sunscreen.

When you leave the necropolis to forage, you may find yourself hunted: that is, in the situation of Opposing Goals. **Be prepared with a strong defense.** For hemmed-in situations, always have an escape plan.

When the pickings are easy, keep moving.

Consolidate your alliances to prevent contentious situations. We're all on the same team: Team Z!

Always bestow a reward on one who returns with a fresh kill—he should receive the best of the BRRRAAAIIINNNS. So are the Undead conditioned to strive for the good of the group.

Block all routes of egress for the Mortals. This is known as the Cinema Stratagem. While the Living take in a "Zombie" film at the local multiplex and gorge themselves on corn products, have your lieutenants seal off the exits. Enter the theater under the cover of darkness and in the guise of "*cinéma vérité.*"

In this, the battle is not always to the fleet of foot or intellect (thank evilness for that!), but to the Zombie who waits, watches, and makes the most of every opportunity.

SO MUCH FOR SITUATIONS.

twelve

FIRE

When they are
engulfed in flames

Sun-Tzumbie said: There are five ways of attacking with fire.

The first is to burn the Enemy in its camp.

The second is to burn stores. (Gordo's Gun Shop comes to mind.)

The third is to burn baggage trains, baggage carts, and those annoying rolling suitcases that trip Zombies up.

The fourth is to burn arsenals and magazines, especially periodicals devoted to the Living— Boys' Life, Southern Living, Long-Term Living, Mountain Living, Coastal Living, and Vermont Life.

The fifth is to hurl dropping fire amongst the Enemy.

Fire can be highly useful to a Zombie. It's true: You, in your current state, are no longer concerned with having light, warmth, cooked food, purified water, or sterilized bandages. And you're not really worried about predatory animals. Or signaling for help. Nope. It's the Humans who need fire for all these things. There is an old Human saying: "Where there's smoke, there's fire." And there is also a Zombie saying: "Where there's fire, there's likely BRRRAAAIIINNNS!"

You may lure Humans to you with a good old-fashioned campfire. Making one is easy. Even a Zombie can master this basic wilderness skill. Material for building a fire should always be kept in readiness: matches, gasoline, greasy rags, dryer lint, paper (the publications mentioned earlier will do nicely), grass, bark, and resin (a.k.a. tree sap).

Try to build a fire near dry vegetation; perhaps it will spread to inhabited areas, and drive the Humans from their homes. Go ahead—let your fire get out of control. Safety? Let us remind you: This is a Zombie Apocalypse, not a Boy Scout Jamboree!

There is a proper season for making Zombie attacks with fire, and special days for starting a conflagration. The proper season is when the weather is very dry, obviously; the special days are those when the moon is in the constellations of The Colander, The Wall, The Wing, or The Cross-bar, for these four are all days of rising—ahem—Wind. And if there is one thing the decomposing Zombie can do without peer, it's raise Prodigious Wind.

In attacking with fire, the Zombie should take into account five considerations:

🔥 **When fire breaks out inside the Enemy's camp, respond at once with a Horde attack from without.** No one gets out alive! Except you of course. Although you are dead. In a manner of speaking. Never mind.

🔥 **If there is an outbreak of fire, but the Enemy remains quiet, bide your time and do not attack.** The Humans may be attempting to hornswoggle you. On the other hand, they may have simply panicked and died from smoke asphyxiation, the number one cause of death from fires. Blunder in and feast on their BRRRAAAIIINNNS before they are too well done.

🔥 **When the force of the flames has reached its height, attack, if that is practicable.** Just shamble on into the Enemy camp and make yourself at home. They'll likely mistake you for a counselor.

If it is possible to make an assault with fire from without, do not wait for it to break out within. Go ahead—set the world on fire!

When you start a fire, remain windward of it. Do not attack from the leeward side, unless you wish to become Zombie Flambé.

An ill wind that rises in the daytime lasts long, but a night breeze soon falls. Zombies prefer the longer-lasting, Virus-spreading ill wind. Speaking of wind, stay downwind of the Mortals; your aroma will betray your position. Unless, as mentioned above, you're starting a fire.

In every Horde army, the five developments connected with fire must be known, the movements of the stars calculated, and a watch kept for the proper days. And remember: Star sightings attract Humans in droves. Therefore, Zombie contingents in Hollywood, the Hamptons, and Cannes have built-in advantages. Many celebrities are already Zombies (though a number are vegan); this is not common knowledge among Humans. Even so, these stars attract mobs of fans and insatiable stalking paparazzombies, who seek to capture them in trophy photographs.

Speaking of trophies, **Madame Cadavre Exquis** reminds us to consider the headhunting culture. Headhunting has been practiced in Asia, Africa, South America, New Zealand, the Pacific Islands, and Europe. The practice comes from the belief that one's head contains "life force," which becomes available to those who take the head. (Yes, the modern Zombie knows of this life force, too—BRRRAAAIIINNNSSS!) Some cultures also shrink heads, generally because they incorrectly use the hot water setting on their washing machines. But shrinkage has its bright side: Shrunken heads make cool Zombie accessories. In any event, we must never forget that belief in the power of the head drives our enemies to destroy ours! Madame thanks you for your attention.

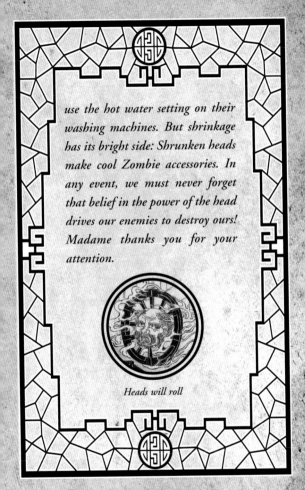

Heads will roll

Hence those Zombies who use fire as an aid to the attack show intelligence; those who use water gain an accession of strength. Fire and water, two of the five elements. It's elementary, my dear Zombie.

By means of water, the Cognizant may be intercepted, but not robbed of all his belongings. But he will know the Human saying to be true: "You can't take it with you!" He will realize that in a Zombie Apocalypse he needs nothing but his—say it with me now—BRRRAAAIIINNNS! (OK, he'll probably be wishing for a spear gun as well, but too bad.)

Unhappy is the fate of the Zombie who tries to win battles and influence people without cultivating the (evil) spirit of enterprise; for the result is a waste of time and general stagnation. Give the Devil his due! Or you're doo-doo.

Hence the saying: The enlightened Horde ruler lays his plans well ahead; the good Horde general cultivates his resources—and his Zombies. Move not unless you see an advantage. Use not your Zombies unless there is something to be gained. Fight not unless the position is critical.

No Horde ruler should put troops into the field merely to gratify and/or consume his own spleen (or another's). No general should fight a battle simply out of pique (or piquant sauce).

If it is to your Undead advantage, make a forward shuffle; if not, stay where you are.

Anger may in time change to gladness with the NOMMING of BRRRAAAIIINNNS; vexation may be succeeded by contentment at least until all available Gray Matter is gone.

But a Horde that has once been destroyed can never come again into being; nor can the dead Undead ever be brought back to, er, Unlife. Or can they? Zom-bie or not Zom-bie…that is the question. (Note to self: Check with Horderatio. And Yorick.)

Hence the enlightened Horde ruler is heedful, and the good Horde general full of caution. This is the way to keep the world at war and Zombies intact, more or less.

NEVER FORGET: THIS IS THE
ZOMBIE
APOCALYPSE.

thirteen

USING SECRET AGENTS

I spy, with
my single eye…

Sun-Tzumbie said: *Raising a host of a hundred thousand corpses and marching them great distances entails heavy losses of flesh and a drain on the resources of the necropolis.* There will be commotion at home and abroad, and the Undead will decompose and rot on the highways. The Living will be preoccupied with clearing away their remains. It is preferable to sacrifice a few of the Horde's more putrid specimens in order to keep the Humans preoccupied with this task.

Hostile armies may face each other for years (We've got all the time in the world; remember? They're the ones who have to dash off to meetings, brunches, and baby showers.), striving for the victory which will be decided in a single day. This being so, to remain in ignorance (a more or less permanent condition for one of Us) simply because one grudges the time and effort, is the height of inHumanity. And we're all about inHumanity. Preach it, Zombie brethren!

One who acts thus is an unnatural leader of the Post Lifers and will bring ruin unto the masses of Humanity. Such a one is devoutly to be wished for. What enables the ruthless Zombie sovereign to strike, conquer, and achieve things beyond the reach of Mortal and immortal alike, is foreknowledge.

Now, this knowledge cannot be elicited from spirits, although Sun-Tzumbie strongly advocates "haunting" the Humans' houses of worship, for these buildings provide a tasty and reliable weekly brunch. Nor can it be gained inductively or by deductive calculations, as the Zombies' mental faculties are usually severely impaired. No, knowledge of the Humans' dispositions can only be obtained from Humans themselves—and BRRRAAAIIINNNS.

Hence, the use of spies.

SPIES

There are five classes of spies:

Local spies

Inward spies

Converted spies

Doomed spies

"Surviving" spies

When these five kinds of spies are all at work, none can discover the secret system. This is called "diabolical manipulation of the threads." It is the Horde's most precious faculty. Let's face it: In a universe of dwindling faculties, one must grasp at every thread (or straw or loose digit).

Having **local spies** means befriending the recently reanimated of a given locale or district.

138

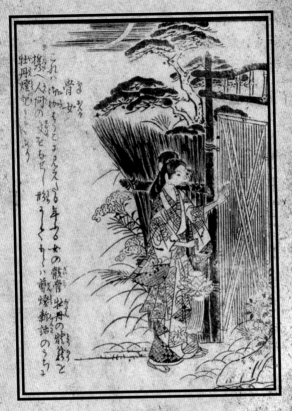

Hone-onna *(skeleton woman) decoy used by Jiang-Shi to lure Imperial warriors into the legions of the Horde*

Having **inward spies** will be difficult, but not impossible. One must make use of the officials of the Enemy. Some law enforcement personnel, especially those living in remote backwaters or rural areas, may be hoodwinked into revealing volumes of information.

Having **converted spies:** Do we really need to explain this? It's not brain surgery. OK, actually it is…of a more primitive nature.

Having **doomed spies:** Select a sufficiently putrefied specimen to infiltrate an encampment of the Living. Watch the results. While your scout may perish, the sacrifice is not without merit, as Mortals will stream in from all directions as ants from an anthill. Forget your scout. He was doomed anyway.

Finally, **"surviving" spies** ("surviving" being a relative term) are those who bring back news from the Enemy's camp.

Hence it is that with none in the whole Horde are more intimate relations to be maintained than with spies.

And none should be more liberally rewarded with choice tidbits of Gray Matter. In no other business should greater secrecy be preserved. Apocalypse Tip: Spies should be coached to use The Moan sparingly, if at all. Always select the freshest-looking of your number.

Spies cannot be usefully employed without a certain intuitive sagacity. This quality will be in short supply amongst the Undead, so choose carefully.

They cannot be properly managed without restraint and straightforwardness.

Without subtle ingenuity of mind (no one said this would be easy!), one cannot make certain of the truth of their reports. You WILL strain what is left of your brain. Count on it. All the more reason for the increasingly aggressive pursuit of fresh Gray Matter.

Be subtle! Be subtle! (Try!) And use your spies for every kind of business.

If a secret piece of news is divulged by a spy before the time (or the spy) is ripe, he must be devoured together with the Zombie to whom the secret was told.

Whether the object be to crush a government facility, storm a theme park, or dine on a particularly troublesome individual (elected officials, religious zealots?), it is always necessary to begin by finding out the names of the attendants, the aides-de-camp, door-keepers, and sentries of the target. Who holds a secret grudge against The Dishonorable Judge Unscrupulous? Who leaves the keys to the executive washroom where anybody—with or without fingers—can pick them up with ease? Our spies must be commissioned to address these questions.

Mortal spies who come to spy on us (let them try!) must be sought out, tempted with bribes and electronic games, led away, and comfortably housed—temporarily. Fatten them up for the inevitable. Thus they will become "converted" spies and available for *our* service.

It is through the information provided by the converted spy that we are able to acquire and employ local and inward spies.

It is owing to his information, again, that we can cause the doomed spy to carry false tidings (and the Virus) to the Enemy.

Last, it is by his or her information that the surviving spy can be used on appointed occasions.

The end aim of spying in all its five varieties is knowledge of the Enemy…and that can only lead to one thing: *More BRRRAAAIIINNNS for all!*

In conclusion, Sun-Tzumbie admonishes:
Of old, the rise of Julius Caesar was
a result of his reanimation by the
Supremely Undead Queen Cleopatra,
of the notoriously Undead Ptolemies.
The subsequent rise of Marc Antony, also
reanimated by the queen before both were
destroyed by Rome, was due to his service
to Caesar. The couple was betrayed by
the spies of the Living who snatched
World Domination from their very
Undead jaws. The fault, dear brutes, lay
not in their stars, but in themselves.
Learn from this sad tale.
Et tu?

Men at some times are masters of their fates. It is up to us—the Undead, the Decaying, the Rotten, the *corps du Corpses*—to become masters of our own, and theirs also.

WE DO NOT SLEEP.
WE DO NOT REST.
WE EXIST TO FEED.
ON BRRRAAAIIINNNS!

LET THE
GAMES BEGIN.

IMAGE CREDITS